Python Programming Techniques

The Art of Coding and Programming Explained

By: Lance Gifford

PUBLISHERS NOTES

Disclaimer

This publication is intended to provide helpful and informative material. It is not intended to diagnose, treat, cure, or prevent any health problem or condition, nor is intended to replace the advice of a physician. No action should be taken solely on the contents of this book. Always consult your physician or qualified health-care professional on any matters regarding your health and before adopting any suggestions in this book or drawing inferences from it.

The author and publisher specifically disclaim all responsibility for any liability, loss or risk, personal or otherwise, which is incurred as a consequence, directly or indirectly, from the use or application of any contents of this book.

Any and all product names referenced within this book are the trademarks of their respective owners. None of these owners have sponsored, authorized, endorsed, or approved this book.

Always read all information provided by the manufacturers' product labels before using their products. The author and publisher are not responsible for claims made by manufacturers.

Paperback Edition

Manufactured in the United States of America

DEDICATION

This book is dedicated to the persons who make technological discoveries every day. We get to benefit from their skill and expertise.

TABLE OF CONTENTS

CHAPTER 1- PYTHON PROGRAMING- WHAT IS IT?

Python is a programming language that is known for its simplicity and versatility. The Python language is known for its high-level capabilities. This leads to clearer programming models while more exact work can be produced.

Planning on Python began in the 1980s and was finalized and began being used at the end of the year 1989. Guido Van Rossum was the main firing force behind the grandiose undertaking. Python was created as an alternative to the ABC language that was popular before Python was created. The original version of Python was used for one decade before the new and improved version of the language, Python 2.0, was released in the year 2000. It was seen as a major upgrade, especially with its additions of a garbage collector and its compatibility with Unicode. The most recent major adjustment of Python came back in 2008 with the release of Python 3.0.

Python features what is known as a multi-paradigm programming language. This means that Python has the ability to support a variety of different paradigms which results in a diverse programming experience in which developers have the freedom to mix and match different styles and paradigms, weaving varied ideas and platforms into a cohesive whole. Python has the unique ability to be incorporated into applications that are already in existence. This is partly possible because of the incredibly compact syntax that the language consists of. The philosophy behind the project includes the idea that there should be an obvious way of doing things, and this is clearly reflected within the very structure of Python.

Python uses a style of typing that is known in the programming world as "duck typing". Duck typing refers to a method that consists of using methods and properties to determine the value of the semantics involved as opposed to other roots of semantics that other programming languages employ.

For those interested in learning the language of Python, there are a variety of resources that can help ease the difficulty of the learning process. Because of its simplicity, Python is generally known as a great first programming language for a beginner to learn. Many computers already come with Python installed. However, if not, it is very easy to install the necessary software to use the language. The installation is even free with PSF or the Python Software Foundation.

Tutorials are easy to find online and can also be accessed, once again, with the PSF. Introductory materials are widespread throughout the web, and many of the resources that are available are completely free. Learning Python can be a huge first step into the world of coding. Python is one of the top most popular languages and shows no signs of slowing down or losing popularity. In fact, since 2008, Python has remained on the top ranked programming languages by coding powerhouses like the TIOBE

Programming Community Index. Several studies on the effectiveness of different programming languages have revealed that Python is one of the most efficient languages out there.

Python Environment

Effective python environment begins with a system check. The first step in using this environment is to be aware of what Python software version is installed on your computer and be prepared to take it from there at any level. In every Python environment, there is a primary operator of the software. This user provides the software backing for the tool and sets the initial requirements.

Setting up Python environment from scratch involves understanding the system needs. Python is available for a wide range of platforms, such as Windows, Linux and Mac OS X. To be more specific, Python is supported by Unix - Linux, Solaris, HP, Sun OS, IRIX and so on, Win 9x/NT/2000, DOS (multiple versions), Macintosh (Intel, PPC, 68K), PalmOS, OS/2,Windows CE, Amiga, VMS/OpenVMS, VxWorks and much more. If you aren't sure of its existence, open a terminal window and type "Python".

Generally, Python is obtained from its official website, where the user can have access to source code, documentation, libraries and binaries as well as the most current update to the software package. The documentation is available in various formats, including HTML and PDF. Installing Python involves downloading the binary code application for your platform type. In the absence of the binary code for your specific platform, a compilation of the source code will do the job. Compiling this way offers more flexibility in selecting the features as well as customizing them.

The installed files get stored in /usr/local/bin location by default. For Windows users, the software must be supported by Microsoft

Installer 2.0 to install correctly. These special installers are not software fault: they are perceived essential for the functioning of the Python by ensuring compatibility with the OS. Someone who understands the flexibility of using Python can easily feel the importance of the installer. By clicking the downloaded file, the Python install wizard will install the files while the user is ready to roll.

The next major step in creating Python environment is to set up the required PATH. The executable files need to be recognized by the OS before performing any task through this software. By setting up PATH, the user is telling the OS where these programs and executable files are found. The path is where the desired named string is stored that is later accessed by command shell or other programs. While Windows and Unix systems require the user set the path details manually, the installer itself handles that task in Mac OS.

Python can be run in many ways. The first method involves coding in the interactive interpreter such as command line. In the second method, the user executes a Python script that automatically invokes the required application on the command line. The third method is through graphical user interface or GUI that the operating system and the Python support. Last but not least, you can also create a virtual environment of Python that allows you to work with an isolated working copy of the software without affecting other projects. In the upcoming chapter you will learn about basic syntax.

CHAPTER 2- PYTHON BASIC SYNTAX

The golden rule of any programming language is to master and comprehend its syntax. This certainly happens to be the first step of any high-level or low-level programming language. Let us throw our spotlight on Python and highlight the syntax that we are supposed to use if we wish to master Python Programming. One needs to be perfect with the rules so that they can make various interpretations of the Python programming language. First of all, the language has to be coded and drafted in such a manner so that anyone who even has bare knowledge about Python programming can easily comprehend what the coding snippet says. Thus, the person who developed the Python language must have definitely aspired to make it easy to comprehend so that it can be used to carry out a wide multitude of operations and functions. Thus, Python Basic Syntax is the set of directives which one needs to take note of if he/she wishes to write a program using Python.

How Python Programming Is Unique Among Other Languages?

It is a well-known fact among avid programmers that Python bears semblance to a few other programming languages such as Java, Perl and C. But this does not necessarily mean that they are totally similar since there are always certain aspects of a programming language which makes it unique among other languages.

Most of the programming languages that have been developed over the course of the past few decades use lots of punctuations as keywords but the difference with Python programming is that almost all of the keywords used in it are simple English words only. The basic syntax of Python has been developed in such a way so that it remains general in nature and simple to figure out.

Basic Syntax Of Python And Its Modes

Python Programming Techniques

There are basically two modes of Python programming and the programmer can choose between any one of the two. First, is the interactive mode programming wherein, the interpreter is invoked by the programmer but without any script file. Thus, in this particular mode, there is no need to pass off any file as a parameter. This function differs for different versions of Python which is why, the programmer is strongly recommended to approach only after knowing the version.

Second, is script mode programming which uses a script as a parameter in order to begin the execution process and this goes on till the time, the program ends its execution. Once the execution has occurred, the interpreter goes inactive.

Those who are interested in Python programming must be well aware of its extensions without which, a program will never run properly. Each and every Python file must carry an extension of ".py" at the end of the file name.

Thus, one needs to know each and every aspect of the basic syntax about Python programming before proceeding ahead, so that they can get the desired output accordingly. Python programming is quite elementary and easy to understand compared to other programming languages.

What Is Meant By Python Basic Syntax

All programming languages have what is called syntax. Syntax is the set of rules that the programmer must follow for the code to work. Python is a very simplistic programming language, with simple to read, and simple to write rules. Instead of using punctuation, Python uses white space for ending lines. Many languages rely heavily on punctuation, such as semi-colons. Python uses colons, and very little else in the way of punctuation. The syntax is simple, and errors will become easier to find with practice. This fact, combined with the intuitive structure of the coding, makes it an easy programming language to learn.

Python is an easy language to learn because of its simplicity. Using white space to end individual lines of code makes it easy to begin programming with very few errors. Often the only punctuation in a given line is a colon, quotation marks, and different parenthesis, and brackets. This is very sparse, compared to other languages, such as C, or Java. Example: print "Welcome to Python!"

This line will produce a line of characters, called a string that will read: Welcome to Python! This is much easier to type out than the same code for C.

#include stdio.h main() { printf("Welcome to C!");. }

Using white space to end lines of code make it easier for a beginning programmer, who often forget things, and encounter multiple syntax errors while writing a program, to be able to become proficient with the language. This creates a following for the language, and helps to keep it alive and going.

The punctuation used in the syntax, and the intuitive way the syntax was designed combines to create a programming language that offers a simple way of doing things. Often there is a one way around a problem. This is convenient and boosts a new programmer's self-confidence. When there are multiple ways to work around a problem, confusion usually follows. When a simple to understand programming language is used, the problem seems to jump out at you.

Finding a syntax error can be fairly daunting, especially when the line of code with the error is buried in dozens of punctuation marks; adding a comment to a line of code is simple, as well. Using the hash tag, (#) at the beginning of the line, you can then write a comment to yourself, or the next programmer, to explain the line. This is much easier than other languages that require the comment symbols to be at the beginning and the end of the comment.

The syntax for the Python programming language is the rules that the code and the coders must follow. It dictates how the code will be written. Python is a very intuitive language, that is easy to write, and easy to read. The syntax does not rely heavily on punctuation marks to end lines of code. There is often only one answer to a problem with Python, but more often than not, it is the most simple way. The syntax makes Python one of the easiest programming languages to learn.

CHAPTER 3- WHAT ARE PYTHON FUNCTIONS AND BASIC OPERATORS?

Python functions are widely used programming languages of the highest level and are used globally. Python syntax is so designed that programmers can use fewer lines of codes for expressing concepts as opposed to languages like C. It provides constructs for enabling clear programs on both large and small scales.

Python functions support numerous programming paradigms including imperative, object-oriented and functional styles. It has a dynamic system and memory management is automatic. It is often used as scripting language, similar to any other dynamic language. However, the difference lies in the fact that Python functions can also be used in various non-scripting contexts. It is possible to package Python code in separate executable programs by means of third-party tools.

Features Of Python Functions

As mentioned above, Python supports numerous programming paradigms. It supports structured and object oriented programming. Numerous features of the language also support functional and aspect oriented programming.

An essential feature of Python functions is late binding or name resolution that binds variable names and methods at the time of execution of the program; only limited support is offered. Here is a list of useful python features and functions:

- Defining Functions with Arbitrary Number of Arguments – Most people are aware that Python allows function defining using optional arguments. But not many people know that a method exists that allows arbitrary number of function arguments.
- Finding Files Using Glob() – Most Python functions have description and very long names and unless you are familiar with the term Glob(), it would not be possible to explain what it is. To keep it short, understand that is a more capable version of listdir() function, allowing you to find files making use of patterns. You can find numerous file types. To get each file's full path, just call realpath() function.
- Debugging – The inspect module is extremely useful for debugging purposes.
- Unique ID Generation – Many times, you may find the need for generating a unique string. Although not meant for the purpose, people make use of md5() function. Python function uuid() is meant for this specific purpose of unique ID generation. The strings so generated will be unique but will still have some similarity after some characters. The reason for this is related to the network address of the computer.

Serialization- Python has functions that help you convert objects or arrays to formatted strings. Storing text files or complex variables in a database is just that easy.

Registering Shutdown Functions- A module, known as atexit, lets you execute some codes before the script stops running. Suppose, you would like to capture some statistics such as the length of time it took for running after the script finishes execution. You can add the code at the bottom of the script. It runs before the script finishes. Using atexit.register() will ensure that even if there is a fatal error or if the user terminates it, the code will be executed.

These are some of the features and functions of Python that are helpful to all users.

Basic Operators

In order to understand what Python basic operators are, it is important to understand what Python is. In short, Python is used to program computers for a variety of complex programs. Python basic operators, on the other hand, are the ways in which the programs are written. There are several different types of basic operators that are utilized in Python programming. These are identity operators, membership operators, bitwise operators, logical operators, assignment operators, comparison operators and arithmetic operators.

Identity operators essentially compare the locations of objects. Usually it is a comparison between two objects. Examples of identity operators are "is not" and "is." The positive form of this operator is designed to evaluate variables that are true while the negative form evaluates variables that are false. Membership operators, on the other hand, are typically used for lists that include several different directions or commands. The "in" operator is utilized to program commands that are true, while "not in" does exactly the opposite.

Logical operators are based on some type of variable and are used to program a number of different commands within the Python language. Examples of these commands are "and," "or" and "not." It will depend on the language that is being written into the program as to which commands will be used. Bitwise operators are exactly what they sound like, and operate exclusively based on bits. There are several commands which are utilized with bitwise operators and everything is based on a specific operation that is conducted using a bit by bit strategy.

Similarly, Assignment operators utilize variables in order to create a type of language that can be understood by the program. Again, several different commands are utilized for assignment operators. This is one of the main components of the Python language and is used in virtually all programs along with some of the other more specific types of operators that are discussed herein. Comparison operators also work on variables and utilize many of the same individual commands, although the commands will have different meanings when written in this fashion.

Finally, Arithmetic operators utilize a given variable to assume another variable. As the name implies, most of the commands that are utilized when writing this language involve using the signs and symbols that are used in arithmetic. It is a basic component of the Python language and is one that has been used successfully in many other types of computer programs as well.

The Python language is one of the most popular languages in existence. It is used for a variety of different tasks which commonly require a program that can be adapted very quickly. Understanding the purpose of these basic operators will help people gain a better understanding of how the individual commands are written within the Python language itself. As a result, programmers are able to complete programs very rapidly when utilizing these basic operators. In addition, the program itself it is one that is able to adapt quickly to ever changing situations and as such, it is typically used in specific situations which require a computer program to do multiple calculations at any one given time where other programs that function at a slower pace may not be as well suited.

Chapter 4- Statements-Making Decisions With Python

There are many things that you can code a program to do. You can make a program hold data. You can make it print statements. You can even program it to make decisions. This is true in many of the programming languages, and Python is no exception. The main aspects of the Python decision making are **if** statements, **if...else** statements and **nested if** statements. By using these statements, it is possible to allow Python to take care of its decision making.

if Statements

This decision making statement is the simplest of the three statements mentioned. It is also the statement that makes the others possible because without the **if** all the other statements can't stand. This statement basically means that if a given condition is true, which is a non-zero or non-null value, then a given outcome will occur. Otherwise, it is false, a zero or null value, and nothing happens.

if...else Statements

This decision making statement is an extension of the **if** statement. By adding the **else** to the statement, it allows for alternative outcomes. These kinds of statements can be used if there is an outcome that can result from a true condition or a false condition. More than that, this type of statement can also be modified to become an **if...elif** statement. By using this type of statement, it allows for situations where multiple conditions can be input and will execute one once it is true. The **if...elif** statement also fixes the fact that an **if...else** statement can only be used for one statement at most because it is able to have as many statements as needed; furthermore, the **if...else** statement and the **if...elif** statement can be improved even more as they can be combined to make an

if...elif...else statement. This type of statement allows for the overall **if** statement to be able to handle true outcomes as well as a false one.

nested if Statements

This is the final type of **if** statement that is used in the Python decision making process. This type of **if** statement is just a simple **if** statement with any type of other type of statement within it, Because of this style of **if** statements, it is possible to construct a statement that is an **if...elif...else** statement that has an **if...elif...else** statement within it. This allows for deeper and more complex decision making as decisions can be broken down into smaller and smaller decisions.

All in all, there is a fairly decent amount of ways to reach a decision in Python. Python decision making consists of a variety of different **if** statements and their use in a variety of ways. By introducing the variety of different statement types, it is possible to make the hardest decision making process simple.

CHAPTER 5- PYTHON VARIABLE TYPES

The first computer programming languages set the standards for the discipline. But many of them add on so many widgets that they can be overly complicated and a burden to read. Innovators create "niche" programming languages fulfilling a special attribute, characteristic or feature, such as simplicity. One of the primary goals of the Python computer language has been to create an easier, simpler programming language.

"Benevolent Dictator For Life" Of Python

As mentioned in Chapter 1, in the 1990s, Guido Van Rossum created the Python programming language emphasizing code that was "easier-to-read" due to "fewer lines." He was able to build upon the features and experiences of other languages, like C/C++. Python has "less-cluttered grammar" concentrating on the "obvious way to do something." In a poll comparing the top 5 programming languages for first-time programmers, Python was rated the "easiest to learn" with 34% of the vote.

Python is an interactive, object-oriented, imperative or functional programming language listed under the GNU General Public License (GPL). Python can be used as a scripting language or standalone executable program. Python is a versatile language, which can also be used for multi-paradigm, aspect-oriented and structured programming. Extensions allow the language to be used for design by contract and logic programming.

Python uses dynamic name resolution (late binding) and reference counting. The cycle-detecting garbage collector maximizes computer resources for memory management. Python is installed on all Apple computers running Mac OS X. PySol is a very popular solitaire game using the Python computer language.

What are Python Variable Types?

Computers allocate memory based on need. If the operating system does not need to use all of the memory, then it can be used for running active programs faster. The Python variable is like a hanger for your closet. It is a place holder for data of a certain size, format and type.

The Python variable does not need to be specifically declared, but only needs to have its value assigned to reserve memory space. The "=" sign is used to actually fill the Python variables with real values. These are the seven Python variable types:

- Number
- String
- List
- Tuple
- Dictionary

- Byte
- Boolean

These types are standard for most computer languages. The string is text between quotation marks: "". A list can be modified and is enclosed with square brackets: []. A tuple is a list that cannot be modified and is enclosed with parentheses: (). A dictionary uses defining terms and is enclosed by curly brackets: {}. Multiple assignments are possible in Python. Tuples are discussed in further detail in Chapter 7.

Other Features of Python Variable Types

The subcategories for the Python number values are Int, Long, Float and Complex. Python allows users to convert one variable to another using the type name as a function. Python is well-known for its robust libraries, which increase the interoperability with other languages and operating systems. This library includes a list of types that may be more common in other systems.

CHAPTER 6- WHAT ARE STRINGS?

As Python is one of the most practical and useful computer programming methods, so are the python strings. They are among the most well-known types. Furthermore, there's a lot of information regarding them. This can be useful for many people; especially those who are looking for a simple to use language in industries such as the healthcare, retail and manufacturing industries. Therefore learning how to create python strings is a good starting point.

The python strings are useful in generating customer-specific programming, enhancing the usefulness and creating an easier to understand experience. In addition, they're very easy to create. Characters are enclosed in quotes to create strings. Python treats single quotes similar to double quotes, so single quotes are generally used.

Similar to math, where a value is added to a variable, same thing with python strings where value is added to words. How to assign value to a variable: Variable 1: 'Good Morning.' Variable 2: 'Introductory course for programming'. Variable 1 has two values; each word is a value. In contrast, variable 2 has four words, each word being also a value. The phrase 'Good Morning' forms one string. The results of the values are: "Good Morning' Value1 [0]. Value2 [1.5], where brackets ([) are used to access values on a computer keyboard.

Something important to know is that python strings are immutable, meaning that no changes can be made to the strings once they're created. Therefore new strings are created, representing different values within the program. A good example of this concept is the usage of "how are you", where each word is a string. When building a new string, it takes the three strings and creates "howareyou".

Python Programming Techniques

With numbers, python strings are created the same way, but use the numbers and symbols on a keyboard. For instance, +, -, x, and = work in the usual manner. However, when doing division two forward slashes (//) work best. Example: 24 // 6 =4.

Syntax is a very important component of python strings. Str stands for string literals, which is how the sentences, or newlines, as they are called in programming, are formed. Str can be enclosed using single quotes. To end a newline, a backlash (\) must be used; a string can contain multiple lines, though. Using string methods to form newlines is quite useful. Some string methods are:

- s.lower()s.upper: These return the string's lower or uppercase version.
- s.find('other'): Within 's' will search for other strings.
- s.startswith(other) and s.endswith(other): Will determine if a specific string stats or ends with another string.
- s.isalpha()/s.isdigit()s.isspace(): So strings are in the correct classes of character.

By assigning a variable to a different string, strings can be updated. An example of this is using variable1: 'Good Morning', print "updated string :- " variable1 [3] + day. The result is: Updated String :- Good Day. The [3] in the brackets is the amount of letters forming a value.

This clear explanation answers the question as to what are python strings and will prove most helpful for many users.

CHAPTER 7- WHAT ARE TUPLES

You may be asking what python tuples are. It's a programming tool that many computer techs and geeks as well as everyday computer users use. Python tuples are very similar to lists. However, there is one main difference. One main difference is that one of them can't be changed. Lists can be interchangeable, python tuples can't be. Once you add something to the list, it can't be changed. The same goes for deleting and changing items. Once it is down there, it sticks. So the user needs to be very sure that whatever is on the python tuples is meant to be there.

At first glance these python tuples might seem a bit odd, but there is a reason behind them being unchangeable. Those of you who are programmers are bound to mess up from time to time. Even those of us who are not programmers do the same thing. We sometimes put things down that we didn't mean to put there. Other times, we want some sort of consistency, so we don't really go out of our way to make any changes. Sometimes certain variables end up getting placed on a list, and we need to go back in and delete them later. With python tuples that luxury isn't available.

In other words, a person can't just change a tuple into a list and vice versa. What it boils down to is we need to be direct with the python. We need to be able to tell it that we want to make it into a list, so we can go back in and change things around. Or if we have no intention of changing things, then we need to let it know right off the bat that we want it in tuples mode.

So let's take a look at some examples of what I'm speaking about;

My List Vs. Tuple
My list= (4,5,6)
My list.append (7)
Print (my list)
Tuple
My list= (4,5,6)
Print (my tuple)
Mytuple2= (4,5,6)
Mytuple2.append(4)
Print (my tuple2)
The Results
(4,5,6,7)
(4,5,6)

See the difference, the tuple has no append; if you do try to change the variables in any way, the screen will send you an "error" message. It won't let you do that. Python will bite your head off if you try to make a change and add an append to what you are doing. But let's say, for the sake of argument that you really wanted to test that theory out. Let's say that you wanted to make a change to the python tuple. There is an easy way to get around it. All you need to do is convert the python tuple back into the list mode. From there, you can add in the append change and edit what needs to be done. But for the sake of argument, if you know that you are going to need to make changes, use the "list python" list tool at the beginning.

CHAPTER 8- WHAT ARE LOOPS?

Python is just one of an ever-growing number of programming languages, one with an impressive list of applications. However, the greatest selling point may be the ease-of-use the language boasts; even beginners are able to master Python in a short period of time. A prime example of this is the Python Loop. A crucial part of countless programs; loops are used for a variety of reasons, but how easy they are to write depends greatly on the complexity of the language. In Python's case, one will enjoy not only the simplicity of the programming language's loop but the versatility.

Flexible or not, for one to use a Python Loop accurately, one must first understand what the loop is and its purpose. Generally speaking, a loop is a piece of code that instructs a program to repeat until certain conditions have been met. This is not unlike organizing DVDs, one going through and pulling out the next one in line until the entire collection is compiled in the desired order. In the case of Python, the programming language has two types of loops: a "For Loop" and a "While Loop." Of course, before one can determine which loop best fits one's specific needs, one must first have a deeper understanding of each.

The Python "For Loop" is perhaps the easier of the two to understand, the purpose often just as simple – depending on the overall program. Simply put, a "For Loop" is usually used if one has a part of code one wants to "loop" for a set number of times. This is done by using the "range" and "xrange" functions, the range specifying the number of times the piece of program is to repeat and the xrange returning the iterator, or an object or routine. The most common use of the Python "For Loop" is to extract information from a list, making this loop ideal for things like organizing DVDs.

An alternative to the "For Loop" is the "While Loop", this particular Python code usually used when the programmer has a certain condition to be met. In fact, unlike the "For Loop", a "While Loop" can repeat an infinite number of times or, as stated, until a specified condition is indeed met. This is usually done using a Boolean Condition, or a math equation in which the results are either true or false. Put into simpler terms, a While Loop is like stating that while your coffee is hot, add ice. The condition is the temperature of the coffee, the action adding ice. Once the coffee cools off, one will quit adding ice, the condition met. Needless to say, there are an infinite number of uses for a Python While Loop.

Only the programmer can determine which Python Loop best fits one's needs no matter the programming language's ease-of-use. However, understanding each certainly goes a long way to help. All that is left is to write a program and put good use to Python Loops.

CHAPTER 9- PYTHON MODULES- WHAT ARE THEY?

As programs become larger and more complex, it becomes challenging to track errors and analyze its functionality, but different Python modules can be packaged and easily inserted into programs. A module is a file containing Python definitions and statements.

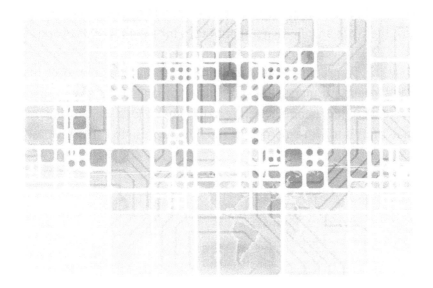

The Advantages Of Using Modules Include:

- Functions and variables must be defined only once, and then they can be used in many programs without writing it again
- Rewrites code
- Allows a program to be organized into several logical sections, each placed in a separate file
- Developers can easily share components

The Python language can be supplemented with many properties by importing modules that provide certain functions and classes that can perform certain tasks. The modules are added to the code by typing import followed by the module name you wish to use.

Writing Modules

Any program you write and save can be imported as a module. For example, if you save a program with the name prog.py, it can be imported using the 'import' command. However, the "import" only occurs once. Python assumes that variables and functions are not changed and the module code merely serves to initialize these elements.

After importing a module the module is compiled and generates a .pyc file. Python only recompiles a program if the .py is newer than the. pyc file.

Initialization Codes

In our modules we can define code that runs automatically when they are imported. If you run the program the first example, the message 'Booting strformat module', which we define in strformat appears.

The rule is simple: the code that is defined in the first level, i.e., outside the definition of classes and functions will be executed as startup module. However, there are some situations where we want our code to run only under special conditions. This is the case of the main modules. We just want our function main () executed if the module is the main. If it has been imported, the application should only be performed if main () is called explicitly. For this, we use the following code:

```
1 if __ name__ == "__ main__":
2 main ()
```

The" __ name__" variable stores the name of the current module. In this case, the initialization code investigates whether the module is the main and performs accordingly. You will find this code very often. It may seem sort of common, but this is the correct way to do core modules.

Packages

When our modules get larger we do not want to have three hundred fifty classes and functions into a single file. We'll want to separate into several modules. That's why packages exist.

What Are They?

Python packages are packages that can contain other modules. In terms of storage modules are structured in files, packages are structured in folders.

Python is a standard library, used for a variety of tasks but there are many implementations of the language such as:

- CPython is the original implementation,
- IronPython is the implementation for .NET
- Stackless Python CPython is a variant
- Jython implementation is for developing in Java
- Pippy is the implementation on Palm
- PyPy is an implementation of Python optimized by JIT

In February 2009 a newer version of Python was developed that included a number of changes that required rewriting earlier codes. To facilitate this process, Python 3 released an automatic tool to complete a list of changes.

CHAPTER 10- EXCEPTIONS HANDLING

Python exception handling is a way of handling exceptional errors that occur in computer programming. Python handles all errors with exceptions and an exception is a signal that an error or the unusual has occurred. Whenever a program is trying to do something erroneous or meaningless, Python will raise an exception to such conduct. Python exceptions handling takes care of errors.

Error reporting and processing through exceptions is one of Python's key features. Python exceptions handling is usually done with a 'try-except' block. It is done to catch all errors that could possibly be generated by a program. When an error occurs with the 'try' block, Python looks for a matching 'except' block to handle it, when one is found, execution jumps there. This means that an exception type always has to be specified to avoid catching all exceptions. All the errors are not always caught sometimes though.

Exception handling is a construct in some programming languages that automatically handles or deals with errors. Some of the programming languages are Java, C++, Python, PHP, objective-C, Ruby, and so many others. All these programs have built-in support for exception handling. So basically Python exception handling is a way of correcting an error that could occur unexpectedly while running a program.

Error handling is generally resolved by saving the state of execution at the very moment the error occurs and to subsequently interrupts the normal flow of the program to execute a special function or a piece of code known as the execution handler. Exception handling in Python is very similar to that of Java, save that the code which harbors the risk of an exception is embedded in a try block.

Two examples of errors that could occur, that Python exception handling fixes are; file open error and division by zero. The program is resumed from previously saved data once the error handler fixes the problems. There are statements introduced by an 'except' keyword in Python with which it is possible to create custom made exceptions. It is also possible to force a specified exception to occur.

It must be noted too that care should be taken with handling exceptions to ensure proper application clean up while still maintaining useful error reporting. A programmer can raise an exception at any time in Python. When this is done, program execution is always interrupted for the interpreter searches to back up the stack to find a context with an exception handler. The search algorithm allows error handling to be organized cleanly in a central or high level place within the program structure.

Python provides robust exception handling and every programmer has to learn exception handling because of the important role it plays in programming. Python exception handling allows programmers to either continue their program or terminate the application after an exception has occurred. Exception information is always needed for debugging. Python exception handling is essential for error fixing in the programming world and it is one out of many others that are used.

ABOUT THE AUTHOR

Lance Gifford did not start out as a programmer; in fact he was not even in the field at all. He specialized in foreign languages but was somehow drawn to computer programming so in his spare time he started to learn the basics of various programming languages like Java, XML and Python. It was python programming that he really liked though so he spent more time learning about that.

Soon Lance was extremely proficient at it and could now start to share his knowledge with others. His latest project resulted in the creation of a book that would help the novice to understand more about the inner workings of python programming.

Lightning Source UK Ltd.
Milton Keynes UK
UKHW02f2140120318
319305UK00008B/767/P